# Tumbalalaika

*a collection of poems*
*by*
## Diana Ayton-Shenker

Narcissus Publications, New York

# Acknowledgments

Several of the poems in this collection were previously published: *Volcanoes (Chaminade Literary Review), The Uncircumcised Jew (Hyphen), I Will Hold You, (Literary Mama), The Old Lover, Land Song (Midstream), Fraulein on a Train (Paris/Atlantic), The Bureau (The Portland Review), The Bee Sting, Coming of Age (Shemom), calamares en su propia tinta (Slipstream), The Fledgling (Spire), There Are People, Tel Aviv Seasons (Tamaqua),* and *City of Peace (Tel Aviv University English literary journal).*

ISBN: 978-0-6151-7842-4

FIRST EDITION

# Tumbalalaika

# CONTENTS

# I.
## Tumbalalaika

## Tumbalalaika

I remember what I found there
cemeteries, memorials, death camps
and temples converted into museums
for the curious, the foreign, the lost
and lonely travelers passing through.

It is true what they say about Jews.
Each generation is chosen to survive.
For five thousand, seven hundred and
fifty-five years we have wandered
exchanging one wilderness for another.

Well, I've been to Auschwitz
and I heard birds sing
incongruous harmonies flew
above the white-flecked earth
whose calcium-saturated dirt remains
unable to absorb the skeletons of its past.

I've been through the *Rynek Glowny*
under the glare of July's red eye
instinctively letting my feet recall
the grey of cobblestone streets
hidden within buried blood lines
an ancestral map written with a key
encoded in a dying tongue.

I might not have run at all in Krakow
but fate forced me to face then flee
a scene of unbridled brutality
one man attacking another
just three yards before me
the victim's head cracked open on pavement
the other leaned over his prey
then looked up to find my fear-filled eyes
and like fear I ran far and fast
darting around corners, losing
myself in the maze of the ghetto
craving to pray before old Jewish graves
I came at last to the garden of the dead
overgrown with mossy head stones
laying strewn in crooked rows
crowded together and soaked
with the blood of this land
this place called Poland
having lost the faintest murmur
of what cries without tears.

## Fraulein on a Train

I look at you and I count them
those lines I fear on your face
the creases of neck and throat
your crow's feet, your brow
the permanent frown tattooed
around thin lips, they whisper
your age and I count them.

You wear those years in your skin
precise as the tracks of railroad
lines defining the distance
between here and there
between now and then
because I need to know
how old you were
when it happened.

I need to see beyond the dark
center of eyes, shiny as black leather
yet worn and weary as the age you wear
in these lines on your face
I need to erase this hatred I see
not yours, but mine.

This hatred I harbor
as knowledge of a secret
crime committed years ago

still dangerous and threatening as fear,

as individual silence, as the collective laughter

I hear in the harshness of your language,

the conductor's footsteps

in the aisle of this train.

and I hate these sounds

as I hate your age,

my silence and fear

as I look at you and I count them.

## Two Mikvehs

The day I visited Toledo
the Mayor and the Sefardi Museum Director
gave me a tour of *El Transito Sinagoga*
exploring excavations and renovations underway.
They led me to an opening
in the ground's dusty floor
revealing a musty cavern
unsealed after centuries
of secret, sacred burial.
Nobody knew it was there. The *mikveh*
was an accidental discovery.
Through the debris of unearthed clay,
I found a large shard of pottery
and picked it up to feel its contours and age.
I stared at that fragment of history
held in my hands for a fraction of time
just long enough to think, "*What is this*?"
when it was no longer mine. I felt it
instantly thrust into calloused hands
who would catalogue, mount and display
this remnant of a ritual vessel
to be seen but never touched again.

There was no water in the Moscow *Mikveh*
when Frida's babushka led the way
down unlit steps hidden behind a door
at the end of a long, gray hall

leading away from the vacant sanctuary
adjacent to the smaller chapel
where I left my father standing
alone with the *minyan* of men
Ashkenazi prayer books and shawls worn
under the shadow of a plaque on the wall
giving praise for Soviet benevolence.
Frida spoke to me in Russian and Yiddish,
I answered in Hebrew and English.
She showed me her *mikveh*,
I showed her my pictures.
*Mein Mikveh; Mein Mishpocheh*
*Bobbe, Zayde, Bobbe, Mameh, Tateh, Elter-Bruder, Bruder*
We sat in the damp, drained *mikveh*
squinting at photos of family,
the thin pages of my *siddur*.
We taught each other *Shabbos zmirot*
and for a little while, we sang together.
Soon after our visit, we heard
the *mikveh* was filled in with cement.


Years later, when I stood with Spanish men
in the Toledo *Mikveh*, I thought of Frida
and silently tried to say *Kaddish*
with a Yiddish accent.

## The Uncircumcised Jew

she bears the covenant
hidden in chambers where life force flows
branding the bond between
her and the ineffable Name

she needs no blade to bleed
knowing blood as she knows birth
born with the weight of silence
soaking through sacred veins of soul

the Chosen Woman
stands whole upon an altar of earth
haloed by branches burning green
flames strong as the sinews of thigh
stretched to the edge of unscarred sex

her voice
whispers true as air
blown through the round of a ram's horn
eternally sounding its fossil curves
sealing the unwritten pact

without a sign
she enters the covenant
binding forever
the uncircumcised Jew.

## Tel Aviv Seasons

In Tel Aviv, I found myself living
surrounded by new and ancient
groves of olive and palm trees
whose leaves remain sandy-green
unstained by the angle of the sun,
the length of days at solstice or equinox.

I had to look to find
the season's changing spectrum
no longer reflected in the foliage
of childhood dogwoods and Douglas Firs,
burgundy, russet and gold-dusted forests,
the southwest hills of Portland.

I found my seasons in Arab grocers'
stands of fresh produce, abundant
and sweetly pungent rows of apricot,
avocados, clementine, guava and grape,
the Fertile Crescent's landscape
of pomegranate, shesek, mango and dates.

These fruits became my autumn leaves,
the quenching rains of summer,
the vernal bloom of crocus,
my snow.

## The Old Lover

We have circled the sun
many times since then, since when
we met when we came together
knowing how we were
growing up and apart.

It doesn't really matter how many
years and time zones separate us,
whenever the phone reincarnates you
your voice fills me with longing
for that innocence, the intimacy
of childhood songs no longer sung.

The first time I heard your voice
you sang *Eycha* in an ancient tongue
solemn as the land where we began
your mournful incantation
resonant of a chanted name.
You came to me as a vision
permanent as the past.

Now you come to me
only in dreams you creep in
between the sleep-slurred words
murmured as whispers touching
the lips that have become my lullaby
my husband lying beside me.

## Land Song

This Land unfolds
its ancient tongue unrolling
to fill white space

as the moon must swell
from right to left
and with light
move oceans.

## City of Peace

Blessed is your coming
blessed as you mount
these hills of olives
and visions.

Royal cats and beggars rule
a divided kingdom of peace.
Think twice
as you may pass them,
avoid their diamond eyes
and curled hand-cups.
Think twice
and pass them by.

Blessed is your coming
blessed are pale stones
who blush as Jerusalem sun
goes down on them.

Ancient walls and ruins wail
in search of multi-colors
once theirs
now faded, foreign,
an exiled body split
in hues subdued.
Once theirs
now black and white.

## Pity Not the Beggar

pity not the beggar
for the beggar still has life
enough to ask the living for bread.

look instead to those too weak
to beg with withered hand,
whose weary mouths and eyes
died bleary in the doom
foreshadows cast
by the holocaust looming ahead.

pity those who dread the warmth
that barely skinned skeletons
give to the not yet dead
corpses packed together in rows
of bones corroding bones,
whose decomposing marrow knows
the stench of heaven's throne.

pity not the beggar
whose pride still lifts his head
enough to look the living in the eye.

## Yom Kippur

The winds chant *we have sinned*
inviting night's cloak to drape over glass
mirrors mourning under somber prayer shawl
shadows cast with shrouds of past
sins we can not starve away
in a day of hunger and thirst
with fists clenched against the chest
pounding the heart beneath the breast
beating sound beyond all human drums
the minor tones of canine howls
wailing how we have sinned.

And the winds whine down into stillness
pierced by the shrill siren of an ambulance
blaring the decades old war cry
moaning in a womb scalpeled barren
irretrievable and irreversibly solemn
as a name erased from a page
replaced by holy verses groaning
the anguish of days unatonable
the fury of promise in a naked new year
awakened with song, *we have sinned.*

## Baptism

fluid heat soaks through the skin
floating within my body
coated in beads of sweat
and sweet bath water.

I dream myself into steam
misting up to rise as tears
contained inside the eyes
knowing only the hidden pink of lids.

I blink and turn face down
half-drowned, half not
I plunge beneath the hot surface
and from my own submersion
my lips blow bubbles of air
flowing up to the atmosphere
absorbed into nothing above.

There are no words.
Sound comes before language.
Air comes before sound.
This is a silent prayer.

# Yahrtzeit

when I pass beyond my days
who will there be to praise
the God I've defamed through worship?
bowing down before false idols
the power of graven images lured me
as the slander of tongue, the names taken
in vain, doubt and adoration of gentiles,
my gentle heathen husband.
who will light the *yahrtzeit* candle
reciting prayer in the dark eve
of my death's annual shadow?

will it be the brother
who answers to the call
my doctor, teacher, rabbi, or father?
will his lips move to speak the words
concealed by a grey streaked beard
whose stains reveal the bitter
bite of horseradish, or the sweet
perfume of white shoulders
the fragrant cloves of childhood?

will it be the sister
whose lover I loved
whose wealth I coveted
who survived starvation
the hands of men, abortions?

will her wounds and womb
have healed enough to grieve
the benediction of mourning?

will it be the unborn future
the generation destined to inherit
this generation's debris?
will my daughters and sons forgive me
the ache of my age demanded
my skin and my bones and I sold them all
except for the blood and the milk
that I saved for them, my children
will they be the ones?

who will hallow these hollow lines?
the blind cadence of the *Kaddish*
echoes the ancient sanctification
of our mortal death and creation
the Divine ruling of a lonely kingdom
ringing with ritual liturgy
before graves and eternal flames
fueled by the praise of this God,
this history, this death.

## II.

## Let's Say We're Old Lovers

## Let's Say We're Old Lovers

Let's say we're old lovers
who've moved on and rediscovered
each other years later, now
married to others, now mated,
the mystery of who we were
destined to become revealed,
the history of our intimacy
already written and sealed
in the shorthand shared by old lovers
imprinted with the memory of each other's
scent, taste, the look in our eyes,
familiar as the sighs we recall
once made while making love. Let's not
say touch me, feel me, fuck me, let's
say we already said that years ago
when we were young, unsettled
unfettered by choices since made
the vows and paths that led us
to where we are now, here
where there's nowhere to go forward
together, only as old lovers with a past
but no future. Let's say it's safe
to see each other, to be friends
and casually embrace and kiss
and confide in one another
as old lovers do. Let's do this.
Let's say it's all over between us

we sailed through that storm
long ago, we rode those waves
and landed safely into separate lives
now reunited, calm and comfortable
as old lovers, at home with each other
once more. Let's say we're old lovers.

## Without Tasting Lips

Without tasting lips
I creep through the dark
hollow corridor of sleep
to follow its lonely stretch
into the space that remains
on one side of the bed
where I struggle in vain
to recapture the senses
your skin, your breath, my own
touch fondling the worn circle
a golden band around my finger
reaching into this hour
it is all that is there.

where is the mouth?
it is silent and dry
when I cry out loud
you do not hush me
you do not answer
I listen but only hear
the echo of my own air
its barely audible whistle
whispered through teeth, not lips.

## La Madrugada

What can I give you?
an hour, an apple, a stone
the lonely echo of my heart
longing to give voice to the secret
part of me, the silence of private
poems and quiet moments that swell
like a reservoir of melted snow
mountain runoffs, rivers, a stream
of tears that well up unexpectedly
like desire, like questions we ask
not of each other, nor ourselves
for fear of the answers we refuse
to hear, such gifts we choose
to ignore for now, the inevitable pull
of what is possible and what is
not, where we are when we are
together, where we are when apart.
I can give you just this:
the promise of *la madrugada*
the pause before our world wakes up
when the darkness is still
heavy around us, slowly giving way
to the first light it will reveal, daybreak
poised to make its gilded entrance
emanating the aura of morning
touching what we share of this time
what I can give you of myself.

## Under The Same Sun

I watch the sun rise
as if unwrapping a gift
hurled through dark skies
from your side of the country
to mine. I close my eyes to be
under the same sun with you
to reach across this red land
and clasp our hands together
from one blue coast to another
I want to call you more than friend
to form new terms of endearment
new words that don't quarantine me
a continent away from where I want to be
with you. I want to open myself
to know you as I feel you
inside, where I hold you
in fantasies, in the senses that stray
beyond the sense of our days
the myriad ways we will never know
each other, never know, though
I'll always wonder where you are
when I look outside my window
framing separate stars and one sun
the same sun hovering above us.

# Flight Home

*"The world in darkness envelops her.*
*Illuminated by a solitary halogen she stares*
*out the portal at her own reflection,*
*flying in a machine she does not understand.*

*Not knowing does not affect her flight,*
*nor diminish her faith and strength of will.*
*The plane flies and she soars*
*an aerialist absorbed by the laws of physics,"*

the laws of attraction that propel her
through darkness, guided by sparks
that flicker between the quickened pulse
of her heartbeat, warmed by the heat
of her breath, the sweet salt of skin
and the flash of eyes glimpsed in the glass
of this mysterious vessel that carries her forward.

She glides her way home, unafraid to touch
down, to find her feet once again on land,
yet longing to remain airborne, floating
above the ground where he stands
transfixed by the laws of gravity
the laws that attach him to concrete, quicksand.
He looks up and reaches out
as if to trace an invisible line, etched
in the night by this new flight path,

not knowing where it leads, but yielding
to its curves and contours, the irrepressible
urge to surrender to the surrounding darkness,
to enter the place where she is, roaming
through territory uncharted, unknown.
He waits and sees her finally
find her way home to him.

## The Measure of a Marriage

It's about the way you squeeze
the toothpaste tube, an elbow,
an extra minute from your schedule,
another ounce of patience, passion
the sheer will to go on another day
another night together, waking up yet
again to the sound of his familiar
breath, the weight of his body
still asleep beside you
and in his sleep and your waking
you reach over and gently touch
the back of your hand to his brow
or softly squeeze his shoulder
before swinging your feet down
from your side of the bed
onto the floor where you stand
and, with care, step
one foot in front of the other.

## 6 rue Portefoin

Inside 6 *rue Portefoin*,
wooden beams stripe the ceiling
hand-painted, mismatched leftover
boards from another century
transported to the end of ours;
two French windows frame
our 2 x 5 metre view of Paris
a rental film of the *Marais*;
nine wooden stairs lead
up to an upper level
where we dress and undress
lie down and rise up together.
These tall, white walls
they hold more than stucco should bear
your art, a *hamsah, mizrach, mezuzah*
the sounds generated here
in laughter, in fear, in private
the cries of anger and love
our first three years of marriage.

Someday, we may find ourselves
sustained by reaching backward
into the spring of our past
the lasting memories of now
looking into each other's face
our skin replaced with old skin
our eyes dimmed from time

and we'll wonder out loud,
*"what was that all about?"*
though we can't return to find out.
For even if we were to return
to find our place together
once again still standing
at this number on this street
recalling what lay beyond the gates
of where we were when we lived
here inside grand, closed doors
sighing, "*Yes, we lived there once,*"
we will be sighing these words
standing outside 6 *rue Portefoin.*

## Waking Up

I wake well-rested, nestled
in the chest of my husband.
Strong arms unfold to enfold me
as a blanket holding me
close to the heart that flows
with the familiar rhythm of us,
of now, of all we bring
to this moment, this bed, this
marriage, the steady beat of a life
shared and built over time
together, as husband and wife.
Outside, a cacophony of morning
sounds beckon: the ornithic song
of birds busy with their own agenda;
a train coming and going to or from
the City; a nautical horn blowing
its greeting to another ship,
passing through our window view
of the Hudson; and from the village
church bells interrupt this sanctuary
with echoes of distant bells pealing
in Paris, Madrid, Jerusalem,
other places and other times
irretrievable and indelible as the shadow
of memory, the vestige of unfulfilled dreams,
the specter of the past, or the false
hope of an impossible future.

Inside, the kitchen clock ticks time forward,
the refrigerator hums, and floorboards creak,
as our son's sleepy voice calls to us
with three-year-old love and certainty:
*Mom, Dad, it's wake up time.*

## In Between

When I wasn't looking
I found you somewhere
between family and friend
you are my love, deeply
held in my heart. I feel you
with me, warm and welcome
as the sun after days of rain.
Come to me somewhere we will find
a home for our love, a place in time
where we can lie down together
at last under the vast, blue canopy
above us where angels whisper
this is where you belong, cradled
in each other's arms
strong and tender
as the dream of your kiss
such bliss touching my lips softly,
sweet as the first day of June.

## Hold me in your eyes and see

hold me in your eyes and see
windy waves of green
seep through eyes weeping
seaweed encrusted oysters
whose pearls remain stones
hiding lonely in shells
longing for luster's coat
to cover crude surface,
as the heart's yearning
to be touched inside,
to be told "*You are*
*the thing which is joy*
*forever,*" for we are
eternal and lonely as air
giving life to be shared
but never owned, knowing
eyes see much more than they hold.

## Three Days

*1. Today*

Every way I turn, I find myself facing you.
Any way I lay myself down,
I dream of being with you.
I am with you when I am with others.
I am with you when I am alone.
My loneliness has a name: Yours. Without you,
I am bereft as winter's deciduous silhouette.
I am undone as the slush of melting snow.
Spring taunts me with its cruel
promise of color and renewal.

*2. Yesterday*

On the last day of winter, I loved you
with abandon. The last time we spoke,
we laughed at how close we were.
The last time I saw you, you were
looking over your shoulder,
out the window, down the street.
The last time I saw you, you were
looking past me. If only I'd known
it was to be our last day
I'd have made you look into my eyes.
I'd have pressed our skin together.
I'd have sealed my hand in yours.
I'd have kissed you more tenderly.
I'd have touched you more gently.

I'd have held you more dearly,
as if holding on for life,
as if it were our last day
on that last day of winter.

*3. Tomorrow*

Tomorrow spring will wash everything
green and alive with the shock
of yellow daffodils and forsythia,
their irrepressible blooms eclipsing
the fading memory of whiter months,
the shifting weight of your absence.
These days stretch forward
rehearsing their sun salutations
as if training for that one long day
the solstice that inevitably will come.

## The Hollow

From the root of my tongue
to the roof of my mouth
I taste nothing but the hollow
of your absence. My heart aches
to be near you, to be calm,
to touch my hand in your hand
my pulse pressed in your palm
feeling the force between us flow
letting you know once more I am
here for you, forgetting all else
to see what you are, for you are
never alone when I'm with you:
this is home. Let our love be
a shelter in the night; a dream
rousing us from sleep; a poem
to answer insomnia's questions;
a sanctuary wherein we seek
and soothe each other; a safe haven
for the sweetness of surrender,
fleeting and enchanting as a firefly,
distant and timeless as a shooting star,
igniting the darkness of these hours,
days, weeks that stretch the memory
of muscles, the capacity of the heart.

## Unspoken

My heart is a sea of forbidden words
the tacit taboo of *I love you* and *yes*,
us, and other unspeakable truths.
I can not wade through their weight
nor fully submerge myself
in the salty waves. I am afloat
in the lap of the Dead Sea
nourished by minerals I inhale
but can not name, awakened by a force
I feel, but can not tame. If we could
breathe soul into memory, I would
infuse these days with a spirit
that rises up as I do when I'm near you
when you look in my eyes and see
more than you know, more than I can say
all that remains unspoken, contained
within the heart, forbidden words
you feel, but haven't heard, from my lips.

## Word Play

I knew from the first letter of the first word
such secrets unheard, hidden within each line
true and straight as a flag pole waving the colors of an
imaginary country, known only in the dream deferred, its
longitude and latitude guarded, never to be revealed
locked and sealed in a vault of unwritten codes

mere metaphors for much more than
I know and feel but can not say
staying clear from all but word play
seeking a way around the censors, the barriers
yielding to the other side of silence
only to find we already hold the key to
unfurl the once buried treasure map

showing how to go forward
onward to that place where
"X" marks the spot.
Oh, if only

desire were so simple, language so true
and love less bitter than
sweet.

## Translation

I often think of you
in another language
whose word for "love"
sounds like a sigh,
*ahava,* this is the sound
my heart speaks to you
when you hold me
when you let go
when our eyes meet
when you're absent
when I am with you
when you are silent
and in your silence I hear
my own pulse clearly, I am
with you in my heart, I am
yours, in any language, *ahava.*

## Snow White

Mirror, mirror on the wall
your face is cold and lonely
a silver box encasing jewels
never worn, locked away from the eyes
of day, the storm of night and silent
vows of longing and belonging
the lingering pull of love
letters shred, poems never read,
words unheard but known by heart
held dearly in reserve
like the truth of what remains
my dream for you to be
love, be loved, beloved.

## Storm Watch

below we count the space
between flash and roar
trembling intervals quicken
with rain licking down
damp, musky earth
pleading more, storm
more from the sky.

electric eyes shriek silent
streaks across the night
lightning's mute beacon ignites
the dark with white sparks
flaring to be seen by sound.

blind thunder's beckoning voice
begs to enter deaf light
clapping black applause
in sky blast detonations
screaming to be heard by sight.

each twists toward the other
imploring to reunite
storm lovers thrash
until two crash into one
shattering flash illumination.

we watch the thunder and lightning

entwine and know the storm
even as it slows to blow
over rain licked earth
dreaming more, storm
more from the sky.

## Between Land and Sky

within yourself you hide
blue-white laser light
ablaze as a single flame's core
you are fire ignited by one match
a spine attached to mine
in the magic of night

the place where two dance
like sun-moon fusion melting
to secret music of silence
sprung from wells of inner tongues
which know no words but taste
sweet drops of rain glossing skin

within you plead to touch
spores that breed tender
beneath green down of fern
nourished by hidden springs
streaming under earth's still surface
rushing into the blur

a dream of the succulent
plucked from one of two trees
whose seeds flow into new
shoots grown embedded between
the other tree trunk's roots
sunk into soil like toes in sand

branches expand and interlace

to reshape the space between land and sky

where man must wander and wonder

until spirits fly releasing the blue-white

light unleashed in air

# III.
## I Will Hold You

## I Will Hold You

While the moon is still high
I hear your cries pierce any hope
of a good night's sleep.
You make out my shadow and
your arms rise up as your voice
calling me to calm you
with the magic balm of Mother.

I whisper I am here, there,
there, it's ok. I will carry you
on swaying hips, hypnotic
as a ship softly dancing on waves.
Let my lips brush your flushed cheeks
let your fever evaporate through pores
let your head rest against my chest
let my heart lull you back to sleep
let the steps of our lullaby waltz
set the pace for your labored breath
let the air flow in and out easy
as the tide of a still and steady sea.

I will hold you
'til the first glint of white
rubs its way through your swollen gums
'til the day breaks free from its nocturnal cage
and the gray light bathes the fields awake
'til the dawn washes darkness from the sky

I will hold you.

I will hold you
while all other souls rest
in the peace of these walls, of their dreams
in this night, I will hold you.
I will hold you
'til your cries subside into the sigh of fatigue.
I will hold you 'til you can no longer hold
the weight of your own eyelids
as they overtake your drive to see
to remain awake and in pain
I will hold you
'til the unbearable strain of childhood becomes bearable.
I will hold you 'til your sippy cup is half full.
I will hold you 'til the needs or nightmares of a sibling
become louder than yours.

I will hold you
while minutes melt hours into days into years
I will hold you 'til my arms can no longer carry.
I will hold you 'til you no longer reach for me
'til you find comfort in the arms of another
or the solace of solitude
until then, I will hold you
I will hold you 'til then.

## The Fledgling

With the first red drops
we heard it, the flutter
of down-covered wings
caught in our chimney
it cried like a prayer
*I am here*
very faint, very soft
secret bird liturgy
calling *I am here*.

When it stopped, we let ourselves hope
and imagined MotherBird had swooped down
to retrieve her fledgling
or perhaps the trapped bird looked up
finding star or street light
to guide its escape.
But when the pains returned
with a steady red flow
once again we heard it
urgent bird whispers
clear as a *shofar*
I am here, *T'kiah, Sh'varim, T'ruah*.

We wanted to save it
to reach through the soot-covered
tunnel between us and the heavens
and hold its shuddering body
in our hands, we wanted to hold

the fluttering, invisible fledgling
to somehow make real
the surreal echo of bird
and we heard it fly
beating wings against brick
with increasing strain
'til the pain grew unbearable
and we closed our ears to the bird.

When we came home from hospital
we lay down under down comfort
side by side in our nest with no words
we listened to the empty chamber of chimney
and found the silence no ultrasound could sense
no flutter, no cries, no bird.

Weeks later, after the miscarriage
I saw it
a single feather in the hearth.
I picked it up, gingerly,
with fingertips tender
I caressed that feather
and brought it to lips
as if to kiss or swallow it
or whisper all memory into it
then I ran outside and turned
my face to the East
and holding the feather
I let my breath go and I blew

very soft, very faint
and I watched it fly away.

## The Second Heartbeat

For five weeks your cells
multiplied geometrically, invisibly
enveloped in silence and hollow darkness,
until you were swallowed up into the void.
I never heard your heartbeat.
Perhaps you sensed my ambivalence
and fear held you back. Perhaps you harbored
some DNA-encoded secret, knowing
with ancient unborn wisdom
our world would not welcome you.
Perhaps you entered a tacit, holy pact
exchanging places with a celestial sibling,
the one who now gives me
my sacred, second heartbeat
pulsing inside along with my own.
In my heart, I know you left me
this gift, my child, you
primed the womb to welcome another
primordial sister or brother,
suspended in my swollen center,
girding strength on the verge
of this journey forward
this new life waiting to be born.
And in this waiting, I heard you
the sound of your soul spoke to me
cloaked in the silence found between
each miraculous heartbeat pounding inside me.

## Coming of Age

At the end of the day
like my Father, I fall
asleep with my glasses on.
My feet swell into my Mother's
feet, the ankles and calves
wear vascular, fishnet stockings.
Her blood pools in my weakened veins
collapsed with the weight of my days
the strain of the unborn
growing inside me. What will it be
that will be passed down
from them to me and mine?
I find myself entering
the age of my parents
in the eyes of my childhood
and I wonder what my child will be
wondering about when s/he's thirty-three,
as my love gently removes my glasses
from my sleeping face, kissing "good-night"
with one hand pressed to the swell
of my belly, caressing the promise
of what is yet to come.

## The Bureau

I recall when my height fit
my mother's antique bureau
it had a beveled mirror
set at a child's eye level
framed in carved dark wood

and when I stood before it
I could stare straight ahead
into that little girl face
encased in the bureau's mirror
then I could see in the dark
looking back at myself
frightened eyes opened
wide as youth, knowing
someday I might not be so small
someday I might not fit
and I must somehow remember

to see those eyes now
I would need to kneel
and fall backwards as memory
reflected still in childhood mirrors
where fears were nothing
more than the idea
someday I might grow up.

## Tuesday

when the world was green
Oregon filled everything
tucked into blankets of rain
sky varnished earth sweet
as blackberry stained fingertips
thorn pricked by divine
fruit lined lanes,

and when there was sun
magic rays illuminated rain light
arcs seen through the prism of air
where soft green swayed
in the shade of silk or weeping
willow tree leaves,

and when the world smiled
vibrant as Oregon green
my face leaned into the warm
embrace of Daddy's chest
the soft breast of Mother,

and it was good
and it was good.

## A Horse Named "Coco"

A horse named "Coco" once
stood in our dining room.
Not while we were there
of course, but decades before
when the house was a stable
and the dining room a stall.
Before the fire. Before the renovation
by the Johnsons who lived there
before us but had to leave
when Mr. Johnson got cancer
and they needed to live
in a smaller place.

We moved in during a January ice
storm that froze all the pipes,
the pine needles, every blade of
grass embalmed in ice. The yard was
a shag carpet woven of crystal shards
surrounded by a landscape of ice sculptures:
sumac, pine, ivy, rhododendron and fern.

It took a week to thaw out
the enormous barn doors,
and equally long to learn
how to unlatch and open them.
Once we mastered the front entrance,
we could come and go as the history

of the stable house itself.
The doorframe was consecrated
to sanctify these passages with words,
an homage to our heritage, our home.

We know its name was "Coco"
from the carving in the wood
of the dining room's sliding stall door.
Nothing else remains of the horse,
no scent, no sound, no ghost.
Only its name and the space it occupied.

Every Friday night we filled Coco's stall
with our family *Shabbos* meal: always
fresh-cut flowers, often salmon-pink roses,
two blessed candles, goblets of berry wine,
*challah* covered with embroidered silk cloth,
heads covered with crocheted threads
and father's hands.

We sat around the lace-draped mahogany table
laid with china and silver trays of
artichoke hearts with melted butter,
asparagus, potatoes, onion and chicken
seasoned with garlic salt, paprika, parsley.
If Coco's spirit ever came to visit,
I hope it was on Shabbat.

I have no vision of this horse,

no stories, no memories, no record.
Only its name survived the fire,
the Johnsons, the ice storm, Shabbat.
Only a word, a name engraved on a door.
"Coco." This is all we know.
It must have been brown.

## Official

That first pink smear, I remember it
in the hotel bathroom for Thanks-
giving Day Weekend at the beach.
I squat-sat on porcelain waiting to call you.
my heart raced so quietly, like sneakers
on asphalt. *Pssst, God, is this it?*
*But it's not red like pricked skin,*
*it doesn't stream like urine,*
*it makes no sound, am I deaf to blood?*
Then I called you in, knowing
how you could sit on the bathtub rim and cry.
You watched me wipe your little girl into woman
shedding caviar, knowing what passed
down through twelve-year-old legs.
You knew and I knew he would, too.
But God, my Daddy, his eyes will look at me
with that Daddy-look and then
it will all be official.
*"Wait 'til I go to sleep, Mom, please!"*
But when I kissed him goodnight that night,
he looked at me, his eyes loving with that look,
and I blushed all that red rushing through my skin.
I cried to my mother, *"You told!"*
and then it was all official.

## Long Island College Hospital

Through the maternity ward window
the 10:00 a.m. light streamed in
to find you and bless you
with a golden December sun kiss
blown across the horizon of your first morning.
You couldn't see her arising from water,
but I caught her gaze of welcome and wisdom
with a wink from the great lady
Liberty aglow in the rosy dawn.
She looked down at your eyes
looking up into mine, you were
cradled at last in my arms,
my wretched, tired, poor arms,
holding on to hope, to the promise
of a new life in a new world,
to the thrill of the unknown
and the calm of landing, holding on
to you, my daughter, you arrived.

## Coming Home After Work to Sarah

Coming home after work to Sarah
the F train full of strangers' eyes
and the cries of a toddler
inconsolable until settled
into his place on his mother's knees
his face half-buried in her cardigan
her chin firm on his head.
I watch them enter that peace
the calm and certainty of their repose
the all-embracing warmth of mother.
I watch and I see in her son
my own child, her head
nestled under my chin, resting
arms over arms, legs over legs
as we rock and rock
in the rickety rocking chair
knowing only this rhythm
oblivious to sound or measure
the tacit poem of mother-child rapture
my daughter asleep in my lap.

Coming home after work to Sarah
I slowly release the tensions
of a day spent raising money
to make sense of genocide
by machete, genocide by neighbors
village by village, televised worldwide

the rape of our daughters, the stench
of the slaughter of a country gone
temporarily insane, reigned by terror
the subtraction of human from inhumane
my own intellectual abstraction
of this nightmare and the mundane
reality of routine, of making money
to support those who make the right kind
of noise, the right kind of gesture,
so that we can rest more easily
in the soft, safe shelter of our beds
wrapped in the arms of our lovers,
our mothers, our delusions, our dreams.

Coming home after work to Sarah
the subway screams me awake at my stop
with the aching screech of its brakes
the doors disappear into the sides of the car
I disappear into the rush hour exodus
an exhausted, automated stampede
of urban, workforce refugees
shuffling onto the platform
anonymous, amorphous, we are
an orderly mob, we follow rules,
we repress the days left behind
unwinding our clocks, the time worn
strapped to wrists, lining foreheads,
defining corners of pursed or smiling lips,
we prepare ourselves for our private domains

funneling single-file through turnstiles
and all the while, we remain profoundly alone.

Alone in our hunger, our appetite, our fears,
alone with the thoughts that no one will hear
alone as a generation of orphans
who witnessed the massacre of their parents
while the world watched on and on waves of air
voiced its concern about the tragedy
of celebrity divorce or weight gain.
Alone as I adjust my shoulder strap, shifting
the weight of unwritten words on paper
work brought home on my back,
as I climb the steps of my own rented stoop,
rising up from the concrete of 96 Dean Street,
where I become Mother, milk maid, lover,
this home where I live and pretend to be
safe with neighbors, friends and strangers
whom I know and adore or ignore each day
as I make my way home to Sarah.

## The Bee Sting

Smiling, I lie to my children again
"*It doesn't hurt*," I say too quickly
rubbing the back of my hand
where the bee sting remains surprisingly
painful as the sting of soap
rinsing out a paper cut,
the sting of the sole
of a foot waking up,
the sting of an old lover's smile
unexpectedly flashed in a dream, a memory,
or on the street where he walks
arm in arm with another
and doesn't see you.
"*It doesn't hurt*," I lie
and massage the red mark
'til the pain is numbed
and I almost believe myself
avoiding their eyes, wondering why
I think I can inoculate them
with another falsehood uttered reassuringly
"*It doesn't hurt at all.*"

## Such Things

At 5:00 a.m. you wake nestled in flannel,
saltwater streaked and strained from wrestling
with God, or angels, or yourself. You
call me for comfort and I find you
standing in blue, footie pajamas
gripping the rail of your crib, while
you wail your steady Mama cry.
You are forlorn, bereft
you have lost your teddy.
In the dark, your hands awoke first
with fingers frantically searching
the void of that still half-asleep space,
groping for soft, fake fur
the familiar nape of stuffed bear,
as your sister carefully strokes
what's left of her bear's frayed tail
and another sister's fingers intimately
re-read the memorized texture of blanket,
fluent in the braille of its weave.
I swiftly retrieve your bear;
it is lying there beside you
just out of reach, and I
pass it to you gently, postponing
the inevitable truth about such things.

Such things we hold dear, the inanimate
companions of childhood, our toys and blankets,

embracing our love and secrets and all
we pour into them. They hold our childhood
fears, anxieties, tears and joy, and we
want to know we can hold them there
close to our mouths, our hearts, our fingertips.
We want to touch this time, this place,
until the hour when we no longer can;
when these repositories of when we were young fade
our curves no longer fitting the curve of their softness
our talismans and dream catchers no longer
warding off the evil eye, the nightmares that will haunt us
in years to come, when we rise again before dawn
to find we can no longer find that place
of comfort, even if we find ourselves
in bed with our blankets and bears,
such things still there, though
withheld beyond our reach somewhere
with no one to help us feel in the dark
for such things when we wake from our sleep.

# IV.
## Under Midnight's Cap

# Under Midnight's Cap

Speak to me like rain touching me
wet down strands of hair
slowly sleeking skin into glazed porcelain bone.

You say, "*yes, what is the moon's pull?*
*I'll know when I see you the third time.*
*I'll watch you like one who sees in you*
*an explosion, vibrant purple charged*
*five times over in five different directions*
*struggling to find a launching pad.*
*I wait to see where you'll take off.*
*You could self-ignite in the rain*
*up, up a lonely mountainside*
*to the moonlit crest where a woman dances*
*like a child kicks inside*
*according to womb walls and rhythm.*
*This is the poem kicking inside you.*"

Awaking, I sigh and see again
through union we find ourselves anew
and fortify vision with irises not found
in fields of isolation and solitude.

We hear voices in rain as in sleep
to wake under midnight's cap
with ears ringing and song hurled to stars.
We taste each other's sweat

to know our own smell

through licks of salty ooze beading from pores.

We touch the print of dog bite gouged in another's footsore

to see we all bear the stamp of paths taken

the stones which stub our toes or rub smoothness into heels.

We delight in ointments and dry cotton gauze

swabbed across each other's wounds

as we know the lines of our own scars,


for in these lines, our lines,

we open ourselves with each other

rising up as a woman dancing

a dance to the moon on a mountain top.

## Autumn Moon

I watch the full moon rise
its smooth ascent reliable
and miraculous as breathing,
undeniably natural and necessary
as magic. I wait for the wolves
to howl in the field. I listen and close
my eyes settling into lunar dreams:
the silhouette of a witch in flight,
overcrowded emergency rooms,
weird coincidences, lovers kissing
on a bridge in Paris, a balcony
overlooking Caribbean shores
of islands named for Christian saints,
a silent climb up the slope of *Masada*.

Hours pass.
I'm startled to wake at night and not
find that round, buoyant face beaming
through my unlit window, its residual
glow diluted by 3:00 a.m. rain, the nebulous
halo hidden behind eerily luminous clouds
backlit by a radiant, resplendent aura,
the moon I no longer see but know is
still there, omnipresent and invisible
like my love for you, inexplicably
durable as the unshakable faith we hold
in a cold and  beautiful stone

suspended in orbit around us
reflecting the fire of our sun
to illuminate mid-October's sky.

# Underground

You've heard there are tours
that go below the surface
you can follow the sewers
underneath the streets
there are tunnels, holes, secret passageways,
a maze of emptied out quarries
massive unfilled graves beneath us
there are musty caves that store
bottled wine and live poets
there are catacombs for the dead ones.

There is a sealed and suffocating river
which flows with poisoned strains
of what remains from 18th century tanners,
the oils pressed from cured skins,
liquid leather waste
there are Roman ruins, well-preserved,
an old church for the pious
residents of our city's buried
playground, an anonymous congregation
non-denominational and sacred.

There are maps to guide you
through this underworld
beware of underground people
who know their way and wait
for you to trespass

into the realm of their rule
they will take your flashlights
they will take your map
they will leave you alone
they will laugh
hideous echoes will haunt you
in the corridors of their home
you will be lost.

You will hear a silence
that grows like a moan
the vacuous underbelly of Paris
aches to reclaim her stones
calculating when and how each building
shall collapse into the rubble
it was before and will be again
reduced once more to ashes, to dust
you must realize beneath this floor
we stand on nothing but history carved strata
layered as an archeological cake
baked in the oven of earth's crusty core.

It is called "The City of Light"
as an omen, a premonition of the flash
that will fill the skies
when Paris falls to refill
its cavernous foundation,
in an instant, urban implosion
of plaster, glass shards, metal,

bone, concrete, and stone.

## Smoke

I want to be smoke
I want to climb up the chimney
charcoal air diffused into choking
lungs of gypsies who sleep
on top of street vents
I want to be black smoke.

I want to be the vocal cords
of a child in song begging
the silent passengers of the subway,
its screeching whine competing
with mine, as they turn away
I want to be a child's voice.

I want to know what it is
to be formless, transmutable
to permeate at will
the bodies that obsess me
my own, yours, the strangers
I want to possess and to know
the strain in a child's voice,
the permanent stain of black smoke.

# The Root of the Tongue

the root is one at its core
in the choke of my throat
division only comes when it tries
to speak, to emerge with words
seeking refuge in the world
outside the inside of my mouth
the slither of my forked tongue
its two prongs twitching
as black wires each
a channel of frequency
charged with law or language
darting out from parted lips
to lick this human body
the aborted fetus, the newborn child
the silenced and the hungry
cry among the corpses
embalmed in serpentine saliva
surviving, wounded and wandering
this aching globe we still call ours.

## The Poetry Reading

Your lips open from inside
out spewing ink spot spit
staining my veins indelibly
yellow as orchid pollen.

Inseminated by your tongue-quill
I sit, tits stand, thrilled as hair
sprouting out from shivering flesh.
I quiver to touch you

where blood moves under skin,
the back of your hand
when it holds a pen, stabbing
again wasp stings through my breast.

I scan and scout the room
landing only on your mouth
not your eyes, bleached hollow death-holes,
but there where I smell soul on your breath.

I tilt my head to view you straight
one lobe nears my shoulder
the other perks alert to air
waves wafting across time

You vibrate into one hundred
ears who came to hear you read

faces melt into space around your words
an onyx blur surrounding stars.

Half a moon blinks away above
us, back to back under separate skies
one darkened east from an old city window
another dimly lit in western afterglow.

I want to color
your blue-black night
with a periwinkle crayon
scribbling there is so much
life between us.

## Volcanoes

do you know, you paint like you speak?
POPping color strokes in sputtered bursts
you stutter pineapples, pipes and definitely-not-pipes
puffed out over and over onto plywood with brush
staining swoops swiping across their surface in arcs
curved like the pucker of lips eating pineapple
or sucking on one of those tobaccoed stems
you paint
everything but the taste of sour
and sweet tropical smoke. In Hawaii
volcanoes must taste like your paintings.

once I stood thigh-deep steeped in Tumwater's weeds
watching Mt. St. Helen's churn and turn inverted
trembling to belch up that perfect lava spout
fired with the force of one of your words
like when you say "*sssshape*" and I hear you
painting shape's form with your tongue
my ears see your sound spoken like paint
translucent hues sprayed on a canvas of air.
the hollow of your mouth knows its words too well
holding them longer to hug them
like the earth's tremored resistance of self-eruption.

I look at your art and hear
you *sssshape* pipe and pineapple
spewed in molten paint combustion.

## Haunted

I know it still comes
the loneliness enters you
slowly, invasive as intravenous drips
whose initial piercing prick
leaves no scar, though
you'll look for it later.

at first you feel
its potent fist shoving its way
through your veins, you bear it
until the pain is tamed
into numbness, a narcotic
sleep without dreams.

afterwards, you wonder
where it began and when
it will come again
unannounced, relentless
it is your secret lover
the one you keep hidden
as an obsession, as a lie
you no longer recognize
I know it still comes.

## Shuddering

shuddering into myself I wake
afraid to open or close
my eyes in the darkness
where screams escape into black
throat-tumor scrapes
grating vocal cords
I would amputate
to release the sound
retrieve the place
where I call to the sky, *I am*
*lonely, only I am alone*
weeping liquid stones that choke me
now those tears only suffocate
stifled inside my cheekbones mildew
soaked in silent condensation
as I open and close
my eyes to find darkness
shuddering around me.

## Heart Ache

There's an itch in my breast
I can't reach, I can't touch
like thoughts of you, buried
heavy and hovering over
my heart like a question mark
begging to ask the unanswerable

*Who are you? What's real?*
*What will I do with all I feel?*
such weight bearing down
worn around my heart
like a chain, like a tumor
in my breast, like the threat
of cells that won't stop itching
won't stop, while I pose
like a good girl, holding still
for my mammogram, the ultrasound
showing shades of grey on grey
the screen drained of all color
obscuring the image into a blur
of what rests above my heart
a cellular mosaic inlaid with fear
of an itch that won't stop
until my hair falls out
and I wear a scar
where my heart once held you.

# Eyes

strain to catch my almond eyes
unshell clandestine seeds
pits hidden by chandelier-clear lids
yours mistake mine as one-way mirrors

you look through my looking glass
imagine the other side
blinded by inside reflectors
deflecting your scan into me

but I do see out to you
squinting through lashes black as ice
there is no mirror to hide behind

only bare transparency revealing
peeled rawness gnawed out exposing
you entranced by the gloss of my iris-shine
the sheen gleaming in glass shells

spell-dazed you stare
ensnared as a spider
stuck up in self-spun lace
your eyes trace what they can't see
pages of dreams, my face

while I glide by alert
blurting out words you'll never

read in lipstick red paint
sprayed across your front door
grinning in naked streaks
stripped for the world to see

## calamares en su propia tinta

the sun blinks
black as dead squid ink
ladled liquid thick
to stain the meat
we eat trying not to
think of the slime we eat

like breathing air in Madrid
what's left of it in August
when heat fills half the life
we live and smog consumes the rest
through lungs we fumigate to feed
fatigued and burning chests

our air turns
black as dead red rose
'til we return to what we know
our parched and thorny stems
pricking into August dust
buried and boiled in our own fuel
*calamares en su propia tinta.*

# The Moth

In these last hours of night
I am not frightened
my eyes dart through this darkness
as a moth in search of light
I fly to the street lamp, a child's flashlight,
Euro-yellow headlights, the ektachrome glow
of an abandoned screen, the addictive
halogen-filled room across the street.
I beat my wings against the glass
but only bruise my alate stem
I can not pass through this window.

Too soon the sounds of dawn
will pound out these lights
drowned in the haze of a new day's sun.
I will wait in the shadows
clinging to some secret corner
my wings enclosing myself
into a camouflaged leaf
so still, so still
I will stay in these shadows
until the ebb of day slips away
into the last hours of night.
Only then will I flutter awake
and fly again through the dark
to the glow, my opium, my halo,
my light.

## The Old Age Home

This is not survival
this is how we die
how we fade away
coddled in the cradle
of mortal decay
reduced to instinct
confined to origin
we rely on strangers
on cushions and carpets
on canes and walkers
our strained olfactory sense.

The others leave gently
vision and sound blend to distraction
static interference, peripheral action
taste blends into bland prunes
rice pudding and custard, pea soup, lamb stew
texture and temperature equally numb
into tepid, tactile anesthesia.

Yet the swell of stale air remains in our lungs
though stained slightly yellow and sickly
sweet with predatory breath
steady, omnipresent incense
pungent as lion to cheetah
as cheetah to fawn

and in the scent of our final foe
we know we consume our own fate
breathing death with each
breath of life we take.

## The Village Woman

When I close my eyes I feel
relief that I need not see
a mountain no longer in place
my barren dreams, your piercing face
the sight of the earth yielding
through voracious fingers, my fists, my claws
myself kneeling before my work

my leader you told me
I would move mountains
I would plough through
I never stopped, not once
to ask for what, for whom
to ask why we need more room
to wallow in a wasteland
desolate as Siberia
desolate as my home, my village
deserted by youth, exiled from sun
those of us who are left
we are old, I am old, I have nothing
to do but sit and take in
the vestige of what would have been

a view of a mountain. Once
there was a mountain
there, I took it down
with my own hands

I took it down
deliberately, efficiently, I conquered
each clod, each rock, each morsel of ore
'til there was no more to take down.

Now there is nothing and no one
will know that mountain, no one will
walk on its slope, no one will
know its contours, its shadows,
no one will know my name.

If someone could miraculously
hear my feeble words
they'd think me insane
demented poor thing, senile, infirm
they'd look away from where I stand
my wizened hand shakily pointing, *There!*
*Right there!* There was a mountain
where now there is nothing
and no one will ever know
what I feel when I close my eyes.

# There are people

There are people who stay
far away from you
though you hear their breath
on the edge of your bed
you feel their heat swell
inside your head compelling
tenuous and unattainable as scent,
as morning's hazy residue of sleep
the wet glaze of an unfinished dream
still wearing imagination's dress
her gossamer skirt barely visible
a filmy caress inside your lids
haunting you with the suggestion of touch
though you know it lies beyond
this time, this awake place of clocks
and coffee and traffic and jobs.

You know they are gone
yet you reach beyond yourself
to hold them again, to grasp
once more the vital pulse
pressed in the clasp of your hand.
But when you uncurl your fisted fingers
revealing your own worn flesh
you gasp at the emptiness
helplessly staring at the silent
lines creased in your palm.

Finally, you release yourself
and seize the calm air
bleeding with palpable absence
you plead, "*where am I?*
*why am I here alone?*
*what do I own of this age?*"
You embrace the sudden rush of rage
awakened to face the threshold and grieve.
Crossing to safety, you weep and gently
retrieve the startling breath of day.

## About the Author

Diana Ayton-Shenker was born in Portland, Oregon, and has lived in Israel, Spain, England, France, and Rhinebeck, New York where she lives with her husband, artist William T. Ayton, and their three children. She is the editor and author of two books about the United Nations. This is her first collection of poems.

### Thank you.

Deep respect and gratitude are due to those trusted readers who reviewed all or part of this manuscript in various draft versions. Their edits, comments, and feedback guided and encouraged me to shape a bunch of poems into this book. I thank those whose work, life and love continue to inspire me and touch my heart of hearts. Above all, I honor my family: Bill Ayton; Sarah Gabrielle, Elizabeth Eleanor, & James William Ayton; Arden Shenker & Lois Sussman Shenker; and Naomi Azrieli.

www.ingramcontent.com/pod-product-compliance
Lightning Source LLC
Chambersburg PA
CBHW030956090426
42737CB00007B/562